Mrs Whippy

Cecelia Ahern

Cecelia Ahern was 21 when she wrote her first Novel, *PS I Love You.* It was an instant best-seller.

Since then she has published two more novels, *Where Rainbows End* and *If You Could See Me Now.*

Cornelsen

Cornelsen Open Door

This edition of *Mrs Whippy* is published by arrangement with New Island Books Ltd.

Umschlaggestaltung
Ellen Meister
(nach Originalausgabe von *Artmark*, Cork, Irland)

www.cornelsen.de

1. Auflage, 1. Druck 2006

Alle Drucke dieser Auflage sind inhaltlich unverändert und können im Unterricht nebeneinander verwendet werden.

Druck: *CPD*, Ebbw Vale, Großbritannien

ISBN-13: 978-3-06-031839-1
ISBN-10: 3-06-031839-5

One

My name is Emelda. Describe myself in twenty words? I can do it in less. There's really not much to me. Forty-six years old. Soon to-be divorced. Mother of five. Five foot three. Two hundred and twenty pounds. Fed-up and mightily bored with my life. Five words that define me? I hate my ex-husband. That's only four words, but you get the point. I tend to fall short of my targets.

I can almost hear my mother in my head.. "Hate is a very strong word,

Emelda. You don't *hate* – you *dislike.*" She does that a lot now since she died. She pops into my head and reminds me to do things. I like it when she does that. It's nice company in my lonely head. Well sorry, my dear departed mother, hate is not a strong enough word for me. I *detest* him and dream of ways he can die a very painful death.

Perhaps that's too evil, but he does deserve my bad thoughts. He deserves my mother to tut and shake her head disapprovingly. She did that when she was disgusted at me. He recently ran off with a twenty-three-year-old Russian lap dancer the size of a broomstick. He left me with five sons: a twenty-five-year-old, a twenty-one-year-old, a sixteen-year-old, an eight-year-old and a five-year-old. The remnants of our once-upon-a-time sex life.

I live in a three-bedroom semi-detached house with patterned wallpapers, curtains, carpets and borders. They haven't been changed since we moved in twenty-five years ago. My kitchen is shabby. My bedroom is a depressing disappointment that, over the years, has seen more depressingly disappointing performances than the West End. Romeo, oh Romeo, my husband was not. Juliet, I certainly am not. The only where-bloody-art-thous uttered from my gob were at four a.m. when he still hadn't returned from a night out. The only standing on a balcony and calling I've done is to hang from our bedroom window while throwing his clothes into the garden. All the neighbours could hear me cursing him.

I was seventeen when I fell in love with the beast named Charlie. "Fell" is the appropriate word because it was indeed my downfall. I remember the exact moment this fall happened. We were having dessert in the cheapest restaurant he could find. We chose delicious vanilla rice-pudding with poached pears and chocolate ice-cream. I looked up from my plate to take a breath from scoffing. I caught his gaze over the flickering flame of the candle. My heart melted like the ice-cream meeting the hot pudding. I can still remember the sweet taste of that chocolate ice-cream on my lips when he kissed me. It was the sweetest kiss I had ever had.

Every moment of my life is marked by ice-cream. I associate moments with tastes, textures and smells. Sweet sugars that pumped into my blood, lifted my heart and made my special moments even more special.

I recall the passion-fruit ice-cream in our wedding cake. I remember it touching my tongue and sliding down my throat as Charlie fed the food into my mouth. My first spoonful of married life. That taste always reminds me of that look on his face. The adoring look that made me think I was the most special woman in the world. I once was in his world.

I remember the vanilla and strawberries on the first night of our honeymoon. I'll never forget how the vanilla felt against my skin as it slid down my stomach and formed a pool in my belly-button while we rolled around laughing.

Knickerbocker Glory reminds me of a time spent watching the sunset on a holiday in Spain. Tones of red and orange decorated the sky over a glistening sea while we watched with sunburned noses and peeling shoulders.

I recall eating mint ice-cream and chocolate Flakes with my mother in the back garden on summer days. I was heavily pregnant, hot and bothered.

The cooling effect of the mint mixed with the familiar smell of my mother's perfume was a wonderful combination.

I remember my father bringing me to the beach as a child and tasting orange Popsicles. That smell brings me back to the sandy beaches, rich with the smell of coconut suntan lotion.

Barbecued bananas and vanilla ice-cream at friends' parties remind me of our "just-married" social life. Vanilla ice-cream between soggy wafers reminds me of the kids' birthdays. Raspberry-ripple-stained T-shirts and ice-cream-and-chocolate-sauce-covered mouths remind me of my growing boys.

All these tastes hold memories.

It's only been a few months since Charlie left me. I do very little these days except sit in my house. I cry and binge on Ben and Jerry's Cookie Dough. Cookie Dough will forever remind me of tears, stinging eyes, snotty tissues and an aching heart. This was my routine until last Monday. After Monday there was a big change in my behaviour.

I knew summer was beginning when I heard that sound – the wonderful tinkling music of the ice-cream van. There was such excitement on the street. Children ran into their homes to beg their parents for money for treats. The music lightened the mood. The day seemed brighter as the distinctive tune played from the speakers. It tickled and teased everyone's senses. That sound immediately reminded me of the smell of barbecues drifting over garden walls. Summer was here. Brightness was here. Hope was here.

I used to feel trapped. I used to feel like I had been stuck down a hole for days with a broken leg. I felt that I couldn't go anywhere or help myself.

The sound of that van was like hearing a rescue helicopter. Mr Whippy was my rescuer. Those tinkling sounds saved me that day.

The man in the van, who called himself Mr Whippy, brought smiles to everyone's faces. He caused parents and children to rush to his side. That man with the twinkle in his eye brought brightness into my life, which had become so dark.

Two

My sixteen-year-old, Brian, has taken to smoking pot in his bedroom. I'm not one of those snooping mothers that roots through her children's things when they are at school. I don't need to. He doesn't hide his habit. He doesn't care if I object. He doesn't lock his door. He doesn't even open his window. No amount of threats of being grounded can stop him. He's sixteen. He's taller than me, stronger than me and apparently knows better than me. So he does what he likes.

My youngest child's name is Mark. He is five years old. Unfortunately, yesterday he was hiding under Brian's bed. It's a new habit of his. He appeared to have inhaled too much smoke. He wandered down to breakfast like a zombie in his Power Rangers pyjamas and cowboy boots. He was complaining that he had the munchies. His eyes were as wide as saucers. He had pupils like Charlie's when he used to watch late-night porn.

Apart from becoming high every day from inhaling second-hand pot, he has now decided that breakfast, lunch and dinner must be eaten under the bed. Whenever we need to leave the house, it takes me twenty minutes to find which bed he has hidden under.

My eight-year-old, Vincent, has taken to not speaking. His school principal has called me into the school twice in two weeks because of his behaviour. But nobody can do anything to convince him to talk.

So I eat dinner practically alone every evening. Mark hides under the bed. Vincent doesn't speak to me. Brian rarely comes home to eat dinner. There's not much I can do about this, unfortunately. How can you drag someone into the house on time when you don't know where they are? How can you force someone to speak? And how can you tell someone to stop hiding when you can't find them?

And I've just realised that each of my boys has copied their father in some form or another.

My eldest son, Charlie Junior, has my heart broken too. He's in prison. He has a sentence of four years for burglary. He's been there for two years. My second eldest, Terry, went on one of those year-long world trips with a group of friends. That was three years ago. He has decided to settle in Thailand. He sends me an e-mail once a month. I don't really know how to work e-mail, so I have to ask Brian to read it to me. He rarely does.

I try my hardest with the boys. I really, really do. I'm a good mother. I know I am. But I can't seem to get through to them. There isn't anyone around me to help. My husband refused to recognise his own bad behaviour during our married life. I doubt he has noticed his sons' carry-on. Any time something was wrong, it was always my fault. He could never compromise. The only time we met in the middle was when we both rolled into the dip in the centre of our twenty-five-year-old bed. If my husband won't listen to me, why on earth would the boys?

My dear mother died last month. My older brother has moved to Ohio. He's opened an Irish store that sells Irish butter, sausages, bacon, chocolate bars, crisps and tea to the homesick Irish community. My very best friend, Susan, is a mother of four and married to a saint of a husband for twenty-five years. She has just begun an affair with the window cleaner. He is twelve years her junior. I feel I can't talk to her any more.

I'm feeling very alone these days. Every day, as I sit on my twenty-five-year-old sofa, I begin to think that it and my life are very similar. It's falling apart at the seams.

Three

My husband takes the boys on Saturdays. I watch him from the bedroom window every week as he drives off in our car. Then I fall onto the bed we used to sleep in together. I stay there until the boys come home the next day.

Today I greeted him at the door. I needed to talk to him about the boys' behaviour. I needed him to back me up more often. I needed the boys to see him support me and respect me. Then perhaps they would listen to me. When all they ever saw was a man that walked all over me, they assumed they could do the same. My mother saw it in them. She tried to teach them. They were as good as gold for her. But as soon as she would leave they would return to their old ways. It was like a bulb being switched off inside me when that happened. My mother was always on my side. I needed the boys to see that Charlie was on my side too.

"Charlie," I said, opening the door before he put the key in the lock. He refused to return the key to what he considered "his house". And it was his. He had never put my name on the deeds to the house. In fact, he had refused to.

He looked up at me in surprise. Then his usual scowl returned. He always seemed irritated by everything I did.

"Where are the boys?" he growled, looking past me.

"They're in the sitting-room," I said, aware that my voice sounded child-like. He had that effect on me. "I just wanted to talk to you about something first."

"What?" he snapped. "We've done enough talking. I'm not coming back. Don't beg me again."

My face reddened. I felt my head get hot. I swallowed hard and looked down at my hands. I still had my wedding ring on. He hadn't. He had refused to wear it the day after he said "I do". I should have known that meant "I don't". I should have known it meant "I never will."

"No, I … I … I don't want to talk about that," I stammered.

"You, you, you what?" He imitated me cruelly. He was enjoying my discomfort.

"I want to talk to you about the boys, Charlie."

"What about them?" He picked at the back of his teeth. When he removed his finger from his mouth, he studied his nail.

"They've been acting up for the past while. They –"

"They're always acting up. They're kids, for Christ's sake." He waved his hand dismissively and looked irritated again. Even when we started going out, I always had the feeling he was embarrassed by me in public. When I began to tell a story he would interrupt and finish it. Sometimes he would make a joke half-way through to change the subject. He didn't like when the attention was on me, when someone else asked for my opinion. He was embarrassed by my opinions. He was ashamed when I didn't agree with him. He belittled me all the time. I said and did nothing about it because I loved him. When I said "I do" at the altar, it meant that I really, really did.

"No, Charlie," I said a little more strongly. "Mr Murphy called me into the school again this week. Vincent still won't talk to anyone. He won't talk to his brothers or any of the kids at school. He won't talk to the teacher. He –"

"He talks to me," he said childishly. Accusingly.

"He does?" I asked in surprise.

"The boys are fine with me. They feel comfortable with me, Emelda," he said. "If they're not happy here, we'll have to make different living arrangements."

I felt like he'd punched me in the stomach. My body started to shake. I couldn't lose my boys.

"Charlie, I think it's important that you tell them to listen to me. I'm their mother. They're with me six days a week. I have to look out for them. I need you to tell them that. I need you to tell them that we both know what's best for them. They should respect that."

He had smirked the whole time that I was talking.

"You want me to do your job for you?" He looked over my shoulder and down the hall.

"Charlie," I continued, "they don't –"

"Boys!" Charlie shouted loudly. He pushed me out of the way and walked into the living-room.

"Listen to me," I continued quietly. I said it to myself, really, rubbing my arm, which had banged against the wall when he pushed me.

"Dad!" Mark yelped. I could hear him jumping up from the floor to wrap his arms around his father.

I tried to control my rage. Every day of my life, everything I did was for those boys. But I never received an excited hug like that.

"Hi, Brian, how's the girlfriend?" I heard. My eyes almost popped out of my head. Girlfriend? What girlfriend?

"Shh," I could hear Brian say.

"Don't worry, she can't hear." Charlie dismissed me and they both laughed. She. He called me *she*.

They left the living-room and pushed past me in the hall. Nobody said goodbye to me apart from little Mark, who was being carried by Charlie.

"Bye, Mam!" he called, leaning over to give me a kiss.

"Bye, love. Be good for your dad," I said, kissing him on the nose.

He nodded excitedly and Charlie carried him away before we could hug.

I watched them walk toward the car. For the first time I noticed that *she* was in the car. The Russian broomstick. The one who swept the ground right from under me. I didn't know her name and I didn't care.

"Hi, Goldie," a voice said as they opened the doors. My heart almost stopped.

It wasn't her name that shocked me. It was the fact that it had been said by Mark. *My* baby Mark. He jumped onto her knee in the front seat and innocently waved at me, bursting with excitement.

My whole body shook and my knees weakened as I watched them all drive off, leaving me in silence. Even at forty-six years of age, I sat on the stairs and cried for my mammy.

Four

As I said already, on Saturdays I usually collapse onto the bed and stay there until the next day. This week I couldn't do that. On Monday I had decided to go out and get a job. Well, I didn't have a choice. Charlie had cut my weekly allowance. When we were married he had felt very strongly about me not working outside of the home. I was happy to stay at home with the boys. Knowing that Charlie wanted to provide for me and the children made me feel safe and protected. I was a very innocent young woman. I handed my independence and life to him on a silver plate. He took it and feasted on them.

I got a part-time job in the local supermarket, packing bags at the till. I could work from eight thirty to two o'clock, two days a week, and a full day on Saturday. I thought it sounded reasonable and that I could cope with it. It meant that I could still collect Mark from school. Brian and Vincent had long stopped wanting to be seen with me in public.

The supermarket was very handy, as it was only ten minutes' walk from the house. But I was feeling very nervous that first morning as I got ready to go to work. I had never worked outside the home. Ever. I met Charlie when I was still in school. We got married as soon as I left. We had children and Charlie felt it was best that I stay home with them.

My first day of work felt like my first day at school. I was going into an unknown environment. I would be surrounded by people I had never met. It was all very new to me.

After the ten-minute walk to the supermarket I was already panting. I was aware I was putting on weight, but I didn't care. Eating ice-cream in the evenings was my only comfort.

They put me to work at a till and, my God, was it busy. I would barely have the first bag open when I would be faced with a pile of groceries. They all moved so quickly off the conveyor belt and gathered at the end of the till. I found it so difficult to keep up. I was sweating after fifteen minutes. The customers just kept on coming.

From the corner of my eye, I could see the supervisor, half my age, keeping her eye on me. Every now and then she would make me take everything out of the bag and start again. Apparently I was mixing dairy with raw meats and squashing fruit with tins. I could barely concentrate on what I was doing. Everything was being fired at me so quickly. All the groceries blended into one and became a blur in my eyes. When I got my first fifteen-minute break, I had never been so pleased to finish anything in my life.

I went into the staff room feeling tired, hot and sweaty. I was greeted by a few giggles. All the other bag-packers were less than half my age.

"You're Mrs O'Grady, aren't you?" one spotty-looking teen said.

"I am," I said politely and pointed to my badge proudly. "Emelda."

"I told you, Jenny," he sneered and they all laughed.

I looked around the room to the girl he referred to as Jenny. I noticed her face was bright red.

"Scarlet," she said, trying to cover her face with the collar of her polo shirt.

"Do I know you?" I asked her politely, looking around the small kitchen for a chair. My feet were swollen and sore, as I had been standing for hours. All the seats had been taken. I could once again hear my mother's voice in my head, giving out about the youth not offering up their seats to their elders.

I flinched with pain as I shifted my weight from foot to foot.

Jenny rolled her eyes and looked away, her face becoming even redder. The crowd all jeered her.

"No one's going to tell me?" I asked, still polite but feeling a little embarrassed now.

They all laughed and continued talking among themselves. Some flicked through magazines, ignoring me. I looked around and spotted a kettle. I filled it with water and flicked the switch. I was absolutely dying for a cup of tea. My arms were sore from the constant movement of packing. I hadn't had that much exercise for years. Leaning against the counter for support, I looked longingly at the chairs. I hoped someone would leave so I could take their seat before I passed out.

Finally the teenagers looked at their watches and began to file out one by one. I spooned sugar into my tea, added a drop of milk and sat down at the table.

"Oooh," I couldn't help but say as the pain disappeared from my feet. I kicked off my shoes and relaxation swept over my body. I took a sip of the hot, sweet tea and allowed it to slide down my throat. It instantly calmed my nerves. I was afraid to close my eyes in case I fell asleep. I felt completely worn out.

There was a bang on the door.

"Emelda!" came the shout from the young supervisor. "Back to work, break's over," she snapped. "There's a line of people waiting at the till."

"Yes! OK!" I replied, jumping and spilling hot tea over my hand. I forced my swollen feet into my shoes. I put the hardly touched cup of tea back on the table and hobbled my way out to the shop floor.

It was only eleven o'clock.

Five

Why do I love ice-cream so much? It's not just the taste I like or the soft, creamy texture. I appreciate ice-cream like a wine drinker appreciates a good glass of wine. Like wine tasting, ice-cream appreciation is not just about drinking or eating it. To experience the true flavour you need to pay attention to your senses. Sight, smell, touch as well as taste.

The colour of ice-cream can tell you its origins. I'm not just talking about brown for chocolate and white for vanilla. I'm talking about rich homemade ice-creams with juicy raspberries, strawberries and blackberries. *Real* ice-creams that don't have artificial flavourings. Ice-creams that don't come straight from a factory and into a tub. I'm talking about ice-creams made in someone's kitchen from organic ingredients and freshly grown fruit, filled with natural flavours. Tangy orange, bitter lemon and country brown bread ice-cream.

Gourmet ice-creams have the right thickness and consistency. The texture on your tongue can be balmy or harsh. Does it give a refreshing zing to the edges of your tongue, enough to make your mouth water? The ideal touch is a mellow softness that leaves a velvety feeling in your mouth. Like the perfect kiss.

When I taste it I take small spoonfuls, like wine tasters take small sips of wine. I leave it on my tongue and allow my tastebuds to get to work. Sometimes it doesn't taste as the aroma leads you to expect. Sometimes the aftertaste is different. Most importantly of all, and the point I've been making about ice-cream, is what is the memory evoked by the ice-cream? Not only on your palate but in your mind.

You've already heard my memories. Childhood days on the beach, wedding days, garden parties, romantic dinners and perfect kisses. Well, I have a new and fresh taste in my mouth to represent a new and fresh memory. Here it is.

I returned from my first day of work and collapsed onto the couch. As soon as I sat down I was sure that I would never, ever stand up again. The more I sank into the couch, the more it seemed to wrap itself around me. It held me tight and hugged my body and I felt loved. By a couch. The phone rang and I ignored it. I couldn't move. I couldn't even make my way to the kitchen for some ice-cream. That's how bad the situation was. All I could feel was shooting pain running up and down my legs, my arms and my back. Packing bags was proving to be very hard work.

Just when I thought that not even an earthquake would move me from my spot, I heard a sound that made my heartbeat quicken. It was the tinkling music of the Mr Whippy van. It got louder and louder as it came nearer and nearer to my road. My heart beat so loud I was sure my neighbours could hear it.

Grabbing my bag from beside me, I forgot my pain and jumped up like a thirteen-year-old who had just spotted Colin Farrell. As I opened the door I saw at least fifteen children running excitedly toward the van. And there he was. Mr Whippy himself, standing at the window, smiling proudly at the approaching crowd.

I joined the back of the queue, feeling like a child. For once in my life it was the man that was having this effect on me and not the ice-cream. What age was he? Early fifties at least, I guessed. He had brown, leathery-looking skin, like he had just been away on holidays. He was dressed in a white T-shirt with a white apron. He had a little white hat on. I could see wisps of black and grey hair sneaking out from under it.

I checked his hands to see whether there was a wedding band on his finger. But he was wearing white surgical-looking gloves. There were no bumps beneath the gloves. Then again, Charlie had never worn a wedding band. So that didn't tell me much. I looked around to see if anyone was watching. I tried to tug my wedding ring off my finger. It wouldn't move. It had been on my finger for so many years it was like a part of me. The fat on my fingers was gathering around the ring, almost cutting off my circulation. I would have to hide my hand from Mr Whippy.

"Hello there," Mr Whippy said to the little girl at the head of the queue.

"Hello." She smiled at him shyly.

"What's your name?" He smiled back.

"Amanda," she said quietly and sweetly.

"Oh, Amanda, that's a lovely name. What ice-cream would you like?"

"A 99 please."

"May I say that's an excellent choice, Amanda?"

Amanda giggled shyly and skipped away happily with her cone.

"Hello, David. Good to see you again," Mr Whippy said to the next young boy. "Where's Matthew today?"

He remembered all their names. I was very impressed. I watched him work his magic with all the children while their parents watched on happily. To the children he was like some kind of god. He was the great big man that owned the ice-cream van that they had to look up at. It was like he was on stage. He was a performer, an entertainer for the parents and children.

Finally, when all the children had received their treats, they went home. Their parents returned to their houses with less money in their pockets. Then it was my turn. I stepped toward Mr

Whippy feeling like little Amanda. Shy and giggly.

"Well, hello." He grinned.

"Hello." I smiled back, noticing my voice was once again child-like.

"I don't believe we've met before." He slid off his glove and thrust his hand out of the window toward me.

He wasn't wearing a ring. I felt like doing a dance.

"Hi, I'm Emelda," I said, taking his hand and shaking it. His hands were smooth and so soft.

"Emelda," he said gently. "Now that's the nicest name I've heard all day."

I laughed. "Charmer."

"Indeed." He smiled.

"And what's your name?" I asked as he put his glove back on.

He raised his eyebrows and held his hands out to indicate his surroundings. "Mr Whippy, of course!"

"Of course." I laughed.

"What can I get you, Emelda?"

He had a lovely way of saying my name. It flowed from his tongue like hot fudge slipping down cold ice-cream. It sounded soft and velvety.

"I'll have the best ice-cream there is," I said, peering over his shoulder into the van.

"Oh. An ice-cream expert, are you?"

I looked down at myself and back to him. "You could put it that way, yes."

He laughed. "That's what I like to see, someone who appreciates my art. Well, let's move away from all this, shall we?" He stepped away from the ice-creams the children had been interested in. "I have some very special ice-cream over here for *true* ice-cream lovers. Can I suggest this freshly made six-layer frozen sweetie pie? Only made yesterday by yours truly. It's bursting with citrus fruity flavours designed to tickle your tongue and prickle your palate."

My jaw dropped. "Yes," I breathed.

"Excellent choice, Emelda."

I handed over my money but he withdrew his hands. "This one is on the house."

"Oh, I couldn't possibly," I began to say, but he cut me off.

"Next time," he said and smiled. "I'll allow you to get the next one, which means I *expect* to see you when I'm here next."

If it weren't for the delicious delight in my hand, and the extra one hundred pounds of fat on my bones, I would have cart-wheeled naked across the lawn with excitement.

I find that the rules of ice-cream tasting are the same for most things in life. To experience true flavours and true feelings you need to pay attention to your senses. How do things look? How do things smell? How do things feel when you touch them or when they touch you? How do they taste? And, very importantly, what memories do they leave you with?

Six

Mr Whippy's ice-cream is not gourmet and it's not expensive. He's appealing to children playing out on the road on spring and summer days. His customers are not people like me that end up with more ice-cream in their mouth than on their faces and on the ground. His ice-cream has none of the richness of more expensive ones. But the lack of exotic flavours is made up for by its preparation.

I can tell this by the look on his face

when he opens the window of the van and serves the children with his biggest, brightest smile. I can tell that his ice-cream was made with love. I know it was prepared with patience and pride. I know that this man's love for ice-cream is his livelihood. I can tell even by one brief meeting that that man has passion.

Later that night, I imagined him preparing his special ice-creams for the next day. I pictured him whisking egg yolks with sugar and salt and moving around the kitchen like he was performing on stage. I could see him splitting vanilla pods and scraping out the seeds. I saw him softly, yet firmly, pressing raspberries and stirring smooth, milky chocolate.

I could imagine the thick, heavy cream gushing into the saucepan and being brought slowly to a simmer. I could hear the small bubbles rising to the surface and bursting with a light popping sound.

I could see him whisking the warm cream into the egg-yolk mixture. I could smell all the aromas in the kitchen. I could feel his excitement as the mixture thickened, the heat of the hob built and his stirring became faster and more constant. All this while he remained calm and didn't allow it to boil. No over-acting; no steps out of place. There was a rhythm to his work.

And then the music would slow as the performance neared its end. He would take the mixture off the heat and pour it into a churn. It would be churned until lovely and thick, the fruit and flavours added right at the end. Then he would transfer it to the freezer, where it would sit until the next day. Work done, song finished and dance completed. It was time to take a bow.

I closed the curtains in my bedroom late that Saturday night. And I felt that Act One certainly had closed in my life. Tomorrow was a new day.

Seven

Usually I would have been in bed when the boys arrived home on Sunday morning. But this morning was different. Feeling refreshed after my meeting the day before with Mr Whippy, I decided to get up early.

I wish I had taken a photo of Charlie and the boys' faces when they walked in the door. They must have been in shock at seeing me out of bed, and that I had dressed myself. I had been wandering around in my egg-stained dressing gown for the past few weeks. Not only was I dressed, I was wearing my finest. I was wearing the outfit I saved for special occasions. Well, there was no point letting it gather dust in my wardrobe. Today was officially a special occasion.

It was the day I was going to take hold of my life. I would once and for all take back what was rightfully mine: my freedom, my dignity and my pride.

"Would you look at the state of you," Charlie said. His mouth gaped open like a fish on ice. His arm was frozen in mid-air from where he had inserted the key in the door. "If it isn't Joan frigging Collins," he spat out, looking me up and down with that familiar look of disgust on his face.

Well. It wasn't quite the reaction I was hoping for.

Brian sniggered. Vincent was silent, as usual. Little Mark looked at me in confusion, as if trying to decide where his mother had gone.

My cheeks pinked beneath my rose-red blusher. Charlie had a point. My best outfit had been purchased for my eldest son's christening years ago. I had spent so much money on it that Charlie had insisted I get as much wear out of it as possible. It was my anniversary outfit, wedding outfit and birthday-party outfit. Here I was, twenty-five years later, standing in my front hall that hadn't been decorated in all that time. It was like some kind of time warp.

I could feel myself bursting out of the bright blue fabric. The buttons were stretching across my expanded waistline. They looked as if they were ready to pop. My shoulders were so padded I looked like I was armoured up and ready for battle. But ready for battle, I was not.

"Mammy, what's in your eyes?" Mark asked timidly.

I thought he was referring to the tears that had begun to well up.

"Eye-liner." Brian smirked and he looked like his father. "*Blue* eyeliner."

OK, so I had gone the whole nine yards. When I had got dressed that morning I had felt beautiful and ready to take on the world. Now I felt like the little girl in *Charlie and the Chocolate Factory* that blew up like a blueberry and had to be rolled off. The more they all stared at me, the more my confidence crumbled.

"Anyway," Charlie continued, marching into the kitchen.

I could hear him rooting through the kitchen presses looking for food, as usual. Nobody noticed how I had scrubbed the house from top to bottom. Nobody commented on how I had attempted to make it and myself look fresh and new.

"What are you cooking?" Charlie shouted with his mouth full of food.

"Breakfast for the boys," I replied wearily, pulling off the bright blue pumps that my feet were squashed into.

"They ate already," he said, appearing at the kitchen door with a sausage in his hand. He dropped it into his mouth and munched it.

"You cooked for them?" I asked in surprise.

"No." He looked irritated again. "We went to McDonald's."

"Oh, Charlie, I wish you wouldn't do that. It's so bad for them."

He looked me up and down again. "You should talk," he jeered and swaggered down the hall and out the door.

I went to the kitchen, filled a plate of food and brought it upstairs. I got down onto my knees in Mark's bedroom and slid the plate under the bed.

"Thanks, Mam," his little voice chirped. "You look funny. Is today fancy-dress day?"

I sighed, sat on the carpet and listened to his quiet munching underneath the bed. I caught sight of myself in the bedroom mirror with my big earrings and my frizzy back-combed hair. My face was painted in orange foundation, blue eye-shadow and ice-pink lips.

I certainly felt like a clown.

Eight

No sooner had the boys returned than the sparkle and freshness disappeared from the house. Their over-night bags had been overturned, leaving their clothes messily draped across the house. Toys, computer games and DVDs cluttered the living-room floor. Their washing piled up in the basket. The ironing piled up on the board. I had taken off my "best" outfit and replaced it with my usual black leggings and T-shirt. I felt completely deflated that my revolt had got me nowhere. I began the ironing while keeping an eye on the TV in the living-room.

Two school uniforms and three football jerseys later, the phone rang.

"Hello?"

"Well, are the remnants back?"

It was Susan, my best friend since I had moved to the street twenty-five years ago. She always referred to the boys as remnants, meaning the leftovers of our marriage. The only proof that Charlie and I had ever had sex.

"Yes, they're back." I brought my cup of tea and cigarette over to the couch and sat down. I knew this would be a long conversation. It always was. Well, at least it used to be before she started seeing the window cleaner. I needed to talk to her. I had so much to tell her and I needed advice. I needed someone of sound mind to tell me that I wasn't as useless as everyone else was making me feel.

"Damn," Susan swore down the phone.

"What's wrong?"

"I'll have to check with Julie if her kids are with her ex for the day."

"Why?"

"Paul wants to take me out for a picnic today, up the Wicklow Mountains. Lately Ray's been asking twenty questions every time I walk out of the house. I need an excuse. But if I say I'm in your house all day then the kids will let it slip that I wasn't." She groaned. "Oh, this is so unfair. Why can't anything good happen for me?"

I was speechless. I just sat on the couch with my mouth open in shock. My cigarette burned down so much the ash fell onto my lap and burned a hole in my Mickey Mouse T-shirt.

"Hello? Are you there, Emelda?"

"Yes," I managed to say. *She* had all the bad luck? She had a wonderful, faithful husband and four saint-like children who all got As in school. And she thought *she* was *unlucky*?

"Never mind. What are you doing on Tuesday night?"

I ignored her earlier comment because of the chance to meet up with her. "Oh, I'd love to meet up. We haven't had a good chat for such a long time. I've so much to tell you. Lately everything has really been getting on top of me. The boys are acting up. Charlie is being *horrible* and this new job I've started is –"

"No, no, no, no," Susan interrupted. "I mean, does Tuesday suit you as a day for me to *pretend* to Ray I'm calling over to you? Paul wants to take me out for dinner. It's really awful not being able to have dates without looking over my shoulder all the time. Honestly," she huffed. "But you would have to promise me that the boys won't be there to say anything. And it would be great if you could stay in for the evening. That way no one will have any proof that I'm not there. You wouldn't believe how people like to talk around here."

I saw red. She made me so angry that my whole body began to shake and my head became hot. I was tired of being used and walked all over by the people who were supposed to love me.

"No, Susan." My voice shook with rage.

"No?" she asked in shock.

"No, you cannot use me as an excuse so you can carry out your dirty, lying, disgusting affair. If you had any sense at all, you would realise that what you are doing is *exactly* what Charlie was doing to me. You saw how hurt I was. You were there for the tears and all the pain. I can't understand how you can do this to Ray. I love Ray. He is a lovely, honest and faithful man. I will *not* have anything to do with this."

"But –"

She tried to interrupt but I wouldn't let her.

"And as for bad luck, Susan, you wouldn't know anything about it. You have a great husband, great children, a great house and a great life. You're so selfish you don't even know what's right in front of you. You ignore those around you, like *me,* for example," I burst out. "I could do with some friendship right now. Don't you dare call me again."

I hung up the phone. I felt good. Empowered.

And right on cue, I heard the magical music tinkling from far away, making its way toward my street.

Nine

I practically danced around the house over the next few days. My latest meeting with Mr Whippy was fresh in my mind. We had spent thirty minutes talking to one another. This time it wasn't just about ice-cream. We really talked. He told me his name was Joe. He was divorced. He had two grown-up children and three grandchildren. I told him all about me. He offered me support and advice. He even offered to take me out some time. A date! I was asked on a date! OK, we hadn't set an actual date, but the prospect of one delighted me.

I'd gone home and gone through my wardrobe. I discarded my "best" outfit, which only a few days ago would have been my immediate choice. I decided that I needed to go shopping. I decided to spend some of my first pay cheque on a new outfit. For once I didn't have Charlie breathing down my neck, trying to make me feel guilty for buying something for myself. I couldn't remember the last time I went shopping just for me. Usually everything I bought was for the boys.

On Thursday afternoon, after my third day at work, Brian returned from school with a scowl on his face. This wasn't unusual, but this time his anger was directed entirely at me.

"Why didn't you tell me you were working at the supermarket?"

I lifted my weary legs up from the sofa where I was lying and sat up.

"What?" was all I could think of to say. I had told him about the job at least five times over the past month. But he never seemed to be interested.

"You heard me," he said rudely.

"Excuse me, don't you speak to me like that," I said calmly. "I can remember at least five occasions when I told you about the job. But as usual you ignored me. What's the problem?"

He shifted his body weight from foot to foot. He looked at me with the same sort of expression as his father.

"You're obviously angry about something, Brian. You may as well tell me what because I'm not going to guess," I said. There was a difference within me today. I didn't care what his problem was. I didn't care if I had done something to annoy him. This time I knew it wasn't my fault. It had never been my fault. That's what Mr Whippy had taught me.

"I've been hearing about you at school," he said a little less confidently. "You're working with some of my mates."

"Really?" I said, sipping my tea. I felt myself become even calmer. I simply didn't care. He couldn't control my emotions any more.

"And Jenny, you've been talking to Jenny. I don't want you talking to her." He tried to sound aggressive. He tried to sound mature and threatening. Just like his great old dad.

I laughed into the cup and spluttered my tea down my top.

His face reddened at being mocked.

"Oh, *Jenny*." I smiled. "I see. Jenny is the girlfriend you and Charlie wouldn't tell me about."

He looked surprised.

"I like Jenny," I said, still smiling. "I was working with her this afternoon. Lovely girl. You know she works three times a week for her *own* money? She's a great girl." I sipped the rest of my tea and continued to watch the TV.

"Don't talk to her, Mam. I don't want you talking to her," he said through gritted teeth.

Vincent had appeared in the hall and was hiding behind the door, listening.

"Why? Are you ashamed of me?" I asked, looking him in the eye.

He looked away. "Why are you working there?" he asked angrily.

"I'm working there because your darling father, who you adore so much, has cut my money. *One* of us has to feed and clothe you. If he won't do it, I will."

"He does look after us," Brian said in defence of his dad.

"How? He takes you to McDonald's on Saturdays? What else does he do?"

Brian stared at me blankly and then spoke. "You won't let us see him any other days."

My mouth dropped open. "Excuse me?" I sat up even more. "That's what he's told you, is it? Well, Brian, listen to this carefully. Your father hasn't even asked me *once* if he can take you another day." I wanted to say that it was my idea for him to take them in the first place. But I didn't want to turn Brian against his father completely. That wasn't my style.

Brian's forehead wrinkled. "You're lying."

I shrugged and looked away, not bothered with the conversation any more. Before Brian left the room, I spoke again, still not moving my head from the television. "I'm a grown woman, Brian. How dare you tell me who I can and cannot talk to! How dare you tell me where to work! I'm your mother and you disgust me with the way you talk to me." I spoke calmly and politely, but with enough strength for it to really hit home.

Vincent stepped out from behind the door. He gave me what I *thought* was a small smile before disappearing again down the hall. The very thought of a smile sent tears flying to my eyes.

After the morning break on Saturday, I was put working on Jenny's till. She eyed me warily for the first thirty minutes. Then she finally spoke.

"So you're Brian's ma?"

I didn't answer. I looked away and waited for the customers to approach us. But the supermarket wasn't busy.

"Hey," she said. "Hello?"

I looked the other way.

"Are you ignoring me?" she asked in surprise.

I turned to her. "My son has ever-so-politely requested that I don't talk to you."

The sides of Jenny's mouth lifted into a smile. Dimples formed on her cheeks. She looked much softer.

"Ah, don't mind him. He's an old grump." She smiled.

My heart lifted.

"What do you see in him?" I asked in confusion. She laughed and shrugged. But I could see her thinking about it.

After a moment she spoke. "He's got nice eyes. Blue sparkly eyes."

"Oh," I said in surprise.

"They're like yours, actually." She studied my face closely. "You've got nice eyes."

"Usually people say the boys look like Charlie," I said, feeling flattered.

"Yuck." Jenny pulled a face. "No way!"

I laughed. "Not a fan of Charlie's, I see?"

Jenny shook her head. "I should ask you what you saw in *him*."

I laughed again. "It looks like you and I are going to get along just fine," I said. "But don't tell Brian," I added.

"Oh, *forget* him." She rolled her eyes. "He'll grow up."

Ten

On Sunday morning I came downstairs to find Charlie rooting around in the kitchen presses again.

"Charlie!" I said angrily.

"You've stopped buying brown sauce." He looked around the press door with a scowl.

I stared at him with anger.

"Why?" he said more forcefully.

"Charlie, you were the only person who liked brown sauce. And you don't live here any more, *remember*?" I folded my arms across my chest.

The boys looked at me in surprise. The child-like tone that was usually in my voice when I spoke to Charlie was gone.

Charlie slowly closed the press door. He stood across from me with his legs spread and his shoulders back, trying to intimidate me.

"How did you get in here?" I asked, knowing that Brian had left his keys behind when he went out with his father.

"They're called *keys*, Emelda." Charlie spoke as though I were stupid. He dangled his keys in front of my face.

I snatched them out of his hand, causing the three boys and Charlie to jump. I put the keys in my pocket.

"Now that you're living with the woman you left me for, you won't be needing *these* any more, will you?"

"What?" Charlie shouted.

"There's no need to raise your voice, Charlie. It's very simple. You have chosen not to be with me any more. You told me you didn't love me any more and that our marriage was over, yes?"

Brian's mouth dropped open. This seemed to be news to him.

Charlie looked at the kids and back at me. "Not in front of the boys, Emelda."

"Why? Afraid you'll look like less of a man, Charlie?" Normally I would agree with him about not discussing this in front of the children. But the circumstances were different this time. His children were imitating his actions because they were being misled. He was not the person they thought he was.

Brian stood up from the kitchen table and cleared his throat. "Da?"

"Not now, Brian," Charlie growled, staring at me.

"Yes now, Da," Brian said forcefully.

Charlie turned to face him in surprise. "What?"

"I was talking to Mam yesterday." Brian raised his chin and puffed out his chest. "And she said that she doesn't mind if you take us to that match on Wednesday."

"Eh … Wednesday?" Charlie said, looking nervous.

"Yeah, Wednesday," Brian repeated.

I was confused.

Brian looked at me to explain. "Da said he had tickets for us for the match on Wednesday, but he couldn't bring us because you said we couldn't go. But you said it was OK, didn't you?"

I tried not to smile at what Brian was doing. Instead I nodded.

"See?" Brian said.

"Yes!" Mark jumped up from the table. He started dancing around and singing about how they were going to the match. My heart broke for him. I didn't like this one bit.

"No, son," Charlie said to Mark, trying to stop him from passing out with excitement. "Calm down. I … I … The tickets are … I don't …" He stopped and looked to me for help.

I shrugged.

Charlie swallowed hard. "I *had* the tickets for you, lads. But when your mam said you couldn't come I gave them to someone else."

Mark stopped jumping up and down. He looked at me with big sad eyes.

"You said we couldn't go, Mammy?"

"No," Brian cut in. "She didn't say no. Da didn't even ask her, did he?" He looked at me. When I refused to answer, he looked at his father. "Did you?" he repeated, his eyes boring into Charlie.

Charlie slowly turned to me with narrowed eyes. I could feel his hate. "You've poisoned them against me," he hissed.

He raised his hand and my hands flew to my face. Brian grabbed his dad's raised arm and shouted, "Get out!"

Little Mark began howling. I dived for him and held him in my arms until he stopped.

There was a long silence.

And then, right on cue, the sweet music of Mr Whippy sounded once again.

Eleven

Mark's eyes lit up. "Mammy! It's your friend!"

Charlie's head snapped around to face me. "Is this your fancy man I've been hearing all about, Emelda? I've heard all about you chatting him up like you're some young one. Are you forgetting who you are and what you look like? A fat –"

"Charlie!" I warned, stopping him from continuing with his insults.

I immediately grabbed Vincent by the hand and carried Mark out of the room. I brought them to the Mr Whippy van. Their eyes lit up and their brows relaxed. Here they were allowed to be children again and to not worry about their parents.

"Are you OK?" Mr Whippy asked, reading my hurt expression.

"Yes." I smiled, his concern touching me. "I am now."

He returned the smile. "Now, what shall I get you boys? I remember you." Mr Whippy looked at Mark. "Your name is Mark, isn't that right?"

Mark nodded happily, feeling very special.

"And what's your name?" He looked at Vincent.

I held my breath, hoping and praying that I would hear Vincent's voice again. It had been so long. I was afraid the scene in the kitchen would have set him back even more.

Vincent looked at me with big, wide blue eyes. I nodded at him in encouragement. He looked back to Mr Whippy and opened his mouth. “Vincent,” he said, so quietly it came out as a whisper.

“That’s a lovely name. Well, Vincent, it’s nice to meet you,” Mr Whippy said softly. “I bet you love 99s like your brother, do you?”

Vincent nodded and said yes. And how I loved the sound of his little voice.

The boys sat happily on the grass with their ice-creams. Joe handed me a chocolate ice-cream cone with butterscotch sauce and sprinkles.

As I took my first taste, I watched as Charlie was forced out of the house by Brian. I watched as he was forced into his car and ordered off down the road. I watched him drive out of my life.

Twelve

When I was a little girl I believed in fairy tales. My mother used to read to me every night while I was snuggled up in bed. I loved hearing stories of princes and princesses who lived in beautiful castles in faraway lands. Just before I would drift off into my own faraway world, my mother would whisper to me that I too would find my prince some day.

Charlie was the first man I ever fell in love with. For over twenty-five years he remained the only man I loved. But when I fell in love with him, I stopped believing in fairy tales.

I believe in them again. Mother, if you can still see me, look. I've found my prince. His white van is the white horse that took him to me. His ice-cream cone is his sword! This fairy tale is real. I have a messy divorce to face and troublesome sons to guide. I have lost a best friend. But I've found my prince and that makes me smile. It's not *where* I live happily ever after, or *who* with. It's the fact that *I* live happily ever after. I know now that's what my mother was trying to teach me.

I have a new ice-cream memory now. Chocolate ice-cream, butterscotch sauce and sprinkles gives me new feelings when I eat it. It gives me the feelings of empowerment, freedom and inner strength. I've learned that the best revenge is finding happiness again.

A revenge of the sweetest kind, served up by Mrs Whippy.

Vocabulary

PAGE 2
(to) **tut** ermahnen
broomstick Besenstiel
remnants Reste

PAGE 3
art-thous
antiquiert: are you (*Plural*)
(to) **curse** (ver)fluchen

PAGE 4
(to) **scoff** futtern

PAGE 5
belly-button Bauchnabel

PAGE 6
soggy matschig
(to) **binge on**
sich vollstopfen mit

PAGE 7
treat besondere Freude
(to) **tickle** kitzeln
(to) **tease** reizen
trapped gefangen

PAGE 9
pot Haschisch
snooping herumschnüffeln
(to) **root through**
herumwühlen

PAGE 10
(to) **have the munchies**
Hunger haben *(besonders nach Drogenkonsum)*

PAGE 11
sentence Haftstrafe

PAGE 13
seams Nähte

PAGE 15
bulb Glühbirne
deeds of a home
Übertragungsurkunde eines Hauses
scowl böser, finsterer Ausdruck

PAGE 17
(to) **act up**
verrückt spielen
dismissively abwerfend, wegwerfend
(to) **belittle**
heruntermachen

PAGE 19
(to) **smirk** grinsen

PAGE 22
allowance Unterhalt

PAGE 23
(to) **feast on**
sich gütlich tun

PAGE 24
(to) **pant** japsen
till Kasse
conveyor belt Fließband

PAGE 25
groceries Lebensmittel
blur
verschwommener Fleck

PAGE 30
tub Becher
tangy scharf
zing Pfiff

PAGE 31
tastebuds
Geschmacksnerven
palate Gaumen

PAGE 33
wisps kleine Büschel

PAGE 37
pie Pastete

PAGE 38
(to) **cart-wheel**
Radschlagen

PAGE 41
whisking egg yolks
Eigelb schlagend
vanilla pods Vanilleschoten

PAGE 45
dignity Würde
frigging *fucking*
(to) **snigger** kichern

PAGE 46
time warp Zeitverzerrung

PAGE 50
the ironing
die Bügelwäsche

PAGE 53
sound vernünftig

PAGE 55
right on cue wie gerufen

PAGE 60
gritted teeth
zusammengebissene
Zähne

PAGE 62
warily vorsichtig,
argwöhnisch

PAGE 63
dimples Grübchen

PAGE 66
press Wandschrank